D0281888

WORLD:
Windsurfing

Paul Mason

A&C Black • London

Produced for A & C Black by
Monkey Puzzle Media Ltd
48 York Avenue
Hove BN3 1PJ, UK

Published by A & C Black
Bloomsbury Publishing Plc
49 - 51 Bedford Square
London
W1CB 3DP

Published 2011
First published in hardback 2010
Copyright © 2010 A & C Black

ISBN 978-1-4081-3045-2

All rights reserved. No part of this
publication may be reproduced, stored
in a retrieval system or transmitted
in any form, electronic, mechanical,
photocopying, recording or otherwise,
without prior permission of Bloomsbury
Publishing Plc.

The right of Paul Mason to be identified
as the author of this Work has been
asserted by him in accordance with the
Copyright, Designs and Patents Act 1988.

A CIP catalogue record for this book is
available from the British Library.

Editor: Dan Rogers
Design: Mayer Media Ltd
Picture research: Lynda Lines

This book is produced using paper that
is made from wood grown in managed,
sustainable forests. It is natural,
renewable and recyclable. The logging
and manufacturing processes conform
to the environmental regulations of the
country of origin.

Printed and bound in China by
C&C Offset Printing Co.,Ltd

Picture acknowledgements
Action Images pp. 1 (Benjamin Thouard/
DPPI), 4 (Benjamin Thouard/DPPI), 6
(Huber Images/Zumapress.com), 11
(Benjamin Thouard/DPPI), 23 (Benjamin
Thouard/DPPI), 28 (Benjamin Thouard/
DPPI), 29 (Benjamin Thouard/DPPI);
Alamy pp. 5 (Nicholas Pitt), 7 (Buzz
Pictures), 9 (Stephen Bardens), 10
(Carrie Bond), 15 (Buzz Pictures), 19
(Bjorn Svensson), 22 (Alan Campbell), 24
bottom (Picture Contact); Funsurf p. 16;
Getty Images pp. 20 (Richard Hallman),
26, 27; Brian Keels p. 14 middle; Danielle
Lucas p. 25; MPM Images pp. 12, 13; No
Zomi p. 14 bottom; Photolibrary pp. 17
(Erik Aeder), 18 (Ingolf Pompe/LOOK-
foto), 21 (Fotosearch Value); Pueblo
Project p. 8; Wikimedia Commons pp.
14 top, 24 top. Compass rose artwork
on front cover and inside pages by
iStockphoto. Map artwork by MPM
Images.

The front cover shows a windsurfer in
action at the Colombia River Gorge
in the USA (Corbis/Richard Hallman/
Aurora).

Every effort has been made to
contact copyright holders of material
reproduced in this book. Any omissions
will be rectified in subsequent printings
if notice is given to the publishers.

SAFETY ADVICE

Don't attempt any of the
activities or techniques
in this book without the
guidance of a qualified
windsurfing instructor.

CONTENTS

It's a Wet and Windy World

You're skimming across the tops of the white-capped waves, your feet safely planted on the **deck** of the windsurfing board. The tail chatters as you race along, spray hitting you in the face. The wind gusts, and you do a little jump, land, and zoom onwards. If that sounds fun, it's time for you to get into windsurfing.

DREAM TICKET
Imagine you have a dream ticket that could take you windsurfing anywhere you wanted, any time! Where should you go? Where are the world's best windsurfing spots for beginners, improvers and experts? This book can help you decide the places that should be on your list.

Is it a bird? Is it a plane?
No – it's an all-action
wave-riding windsurfer.

Technical: Conditions and equipment

Windsurfing equipment is very specialized. There are windsurfing boards, sails and other equipment for light winds, stronger winds above about 25 kilometres per hour (15.5 miles per hour), and different kinds of windsurfing.

Light winds:

• Boards tend to be bigger, with a volume of 135–200 litres (29.7–44 gallons). They float when you stand on them.

• Sails are small – about 4 square metres (43 square feet) – for beginners, making them easy to control.

• Improvers and experts use large sails of 6–10 square metres (64.6–107.6 square feet), to catch more wind and go faster.

Strong winds:

• Boards are smaller and more manoeuvrable, with a volume of 60–110 litres (13.2–24.2 gallons).

• The boards sink below the surface if you stand on them, and are sometimes called "sinkers".

• Sails range from 6 square metres (64.6 square feet) in medium-strength winds to 3.5 square metres (37.7 square feet) in the highest winds.

Specialist equipment:

• Wave **sailors** use short, wider boards, and specially designed sails.

• Slalom and speed sailors use sails shaped to catch as much wind as possible. The speed sailors use narrow boards that slice through the water.

• A harness allows control of the sail in high winds.

THE SECRET LANGUAGE OF WINDSURFING

deck top of a windsurfing board
sailor someone who does windsurfing or other kinds of sailing
kook incompetent person

HINTS AND TIPS

Of course, when you get to the world's best windsurfing spots, you'll need to be sure you know what you're doing. No one wants to look like a **kook**! So we also tell you what each windsurfing location is like, the kind of equipment you'll need, tips from local sailors, and advice on technique. This book is your passport to the windsurfing world!

Rows of different windsurfing boards ready for people to use in a variety of conditions.

Lake Garda

There can't be many places where you can windsurf in warm sunshine, then look up to see snow-capped mountains towering above you. Lake Garda is one of them. Its beautiful location, reliable wind, and great facilities attract windsurfers from all over the world.

LAKE GARDA
Location: Italy
Type of sailing: flat-water
Difficulty level: 1.5 of 5
Best season: June to October

WHY LAKE GARDA?

Lake Garda is over 60 kilometres (37.3 miles) long and over 15 kilometres (9.3 miles) wide at its biggest parts. The coast is made up of a series of beaches, rocky platforms and cliff faces. There is somewhere here for every kind of windsurfer – from beginners looking for a calm lagoon to do some **flat-water sailing**, to experts who want high winds and open water.

Windsurfing on the spectacular Lake Garda in Italy.

THE SECRET LANGUAGE OF WINDSURFING

flat-water sailing windsurfing on a lake or ocean with little or no waves

mast foot attachment between the mast and the deck

Tip from a Local

In July and August, the lake water is sometimes warm enough for sailing without a wetsuit – but the rest of the year, you do need one.

WHEN ARE CONDITIONS BEST?

Beginners: In general, winds are lighter mid-morning, so this is the best time for beginners. The bay at Torbole, at the northern end of the lake, is a good place for complete beginners.

Improvers: In the early afternoon, the Ora wind blows from the south at 25–35 kilometres per hour (15.5–21.7 miles per hour), making ideal conditions for improvers.

Experts: Very early in the morning, the Vento wind from the north can reach over 60 kilometres per hour (37.3 miles per hour) – hard work even for expert sailors.

If you like Lake Garda...

... you could also try:
• Forest Beach Park, Illinois, USA
It has a real big-lake feel.

SKILL
Understanding the wind

The wind and sail together can be used to work out which direction the wind is coming from. Then, by moving the sail, the sailor can change the direction in which the board is facing.

1. Hold the sail out of the water so that it can float free in the air. With your feet either side of the **mast foot**, hold the mast straight upright. The board will swing round so that the wind is right behind you.

2. Lean the mast and sail backwards, towards the tail of the board. The board will swing round so that its nose is pointing into the wind. The further back the mast leans, the more into the wind the board will point.

3. Lean the mast forwards, towards the nose of the board. The board will move round so that its tail is pointing towards the wind.

A wobbly-looking beginner takes her first try at windsurfing. At least the water looks warm, for when she falls in.

Cabarete

The Caribbean has a lot to offer windsurfers. In particular, the warm water and all-year sunny weather make the region very popular with sailors from colder countries. During the official hurricane season from June to October, winds can reach 120 kilometres per hour (74.6 miles per hour) or more. Luckily, this doesn't happen often.

CABARETE
-**Location:** Dominican Republic
Type of sailing: flat-water and wave
Difficulty level: 1.5 of 5
Best season: June to September for beginners

WHY CABARETE?

Cabarete is one of the most popular windsurfing destinations in the Caribbean Sea. All year round, strong winds blow from the east. Beginners and improvers are sheltered from waves by a reef, which forms the outer edge of a large lagoon. The reef is where expert sailors go for the thrill of **wave sailing**.

Tip from a Local

No need to pack your wetsuit – the water in Cabarete is about 26° Centigrade (79° Fahrenheit) all year round.

If you like Cabarete...

... you could also try:
• Kilifi, Kenya
There's warm water and the conditions are varied.

The shallow lagoon at Cabarete is popular with top sailors who want to practise tricks on flat water.

WHEN ARE CONDITIONS BEST?

Beginners: Winds are lighter in the morning, when beginners tend to stick to the sheltered waters inside the reef. Here they can practise in safe sight of the rescue boat.

Improvers: Around lunchtime the wind starts to pick up, and the improvers head out on to the water.

Experts: By about 4.00 p.m. the wind is at its strongest. Expert sailors head out to the reef for some wave-sailing practice.

THE SECRET LANGUAGE OF WINDSURFING

wave sailing windsurfing on rough water, particularly on ocean waves

uphaul rope attached to boom, used to pull sail from water

boom rail attached to the mast, which the sailor holds on to

Once the sail starts to slide out of the water like this, the hard work is done.

SKILL
Hauling up the sail

Learning to pull up the sail is one of the first things windsurfers have to learn. There's a knack to it: if it's hard work, you're not doing it right!

1. With your feet either side of the mast foot, grab hold of the **uphaul** rope.

2. Put your weight on the rope, bending your knees and keeping your arms and back straight. There is no need to pull – just let your weight do the work.

3. As the sail begins to slide out of the water, start to stand up straighter.

4. Leave the far corner of the sail in the water until you are standing up and have your balance.

5. Pull the sail entirely from the water and put your hands on the **boom**, ready to pull the far end of the sail inwards.

Poole Harbour

On a warm summer day, with the pine trees rustling in the wind and the water gleaming blue, Poole Harbour looks more like the Mediterranean Sea than the south coast of England. The area is a hotbed of windsurfing, **kitesurfing** and surfing, so there's always someone around to talk to (and maybe get some advice from).

POOLE HARBOUR
Location: Dorset, England
Type of sailing: flat-water
Difficulty level: 1 of 5
Best season: May to October

THE SECRET LANGUAGE OF WINDSURFING

kitesurfing watersport powered by a kite, with the sailor standing on a small, surfboard-like board

rig sail, mast and boom together

blasting windsurfing at maximum speed

WHY POOLE HARBOUR?

Poole Harbour is one of the best spots anywhere in the world for beginners to practise. The harbour is completely sheltered from the ocean, and large areas are only knee-deep – if you fall off, it's easy to climb straight back on! This is the second-largest natural harbour in the world, so there are plenty of islands and beaches to explore.

These sailors have hopped across to Sandbanks for a spot of open-ocean sailing.

A hard carved turn into the wind, with the mast cranked right back towards the back of the board.

If you like Poole Harbour...

... you could also try:
• Lesvos, Greece
Which has great conditions for beginners.

Tip from a Local

In the middle of Poole Harbour is Brownsea Island. It's famous as a bird sanctuary, and as one of the last places in England where red squirrels survive.

SKILL
Steering

Poole Harbour, with its moored boats, buoys, and other watercraft zipping about, is a perfect place to practise your steering. (Remember, if it looks like you're going to hit something, drop the sail and stop before it's too late.)

• To steer straight across the wind, the mast needs to be upright and the sail pulled in.

• To steer away from the wind (which sailors call "downwind"), lean the whole **rig** forwards. Done quickly, this will lead to a tight turn. Done slowly, the turn will be long and drawn out.

• To steer into the wind, or "upwind", lean the rig backwards, towards the tail of the board.

WHEN ARE CONDITIONS BEST?

Beginners and improvers: Poole Harbour isn't usually too windy for beginners, but the breeze often picks up in the afternoon. This makes it harder for complete beginners to steer around the moored boats – but more fun for improvers.

Experts: Experts will enjoy **blasting** across the harbour at high speed. Or they can do some wave sailing on the ocean off Sandbanks Beach.

The Speed World Cup

Imagine a windsurfer travelling so quickly that he or she could overtake traffic in the slow lane. At a Speed World Cup event, that's just what you can see. Across Europe in the spring and summer, there's a good chance to watch some of the fastest sailors in the world up close, at a series of contests called the Speed World Cup.

THE SPEED WORLD CUP
Location: worldwide
Type of sailing: speed
Difficulty level: 5 of 5
Best season: all year

SPEED-SAILING CONTESTS

The Speed World Cup is open to all kinds of sail-powered craft. As well as windsurfing boards, there are sailboats and kitesurfers. The racers are timed over a straight-line, 500-metre (1640-foot) long course, and can reach speeds of over 90 kilometres per hour (56 miles per hour). In windsurfing, the sailors use huge sails of 10 square metres (107.6 square feet) and narrow boards.

Great technique for wringing maximum speed from a board: the gap between the foot of the sail and the deck is closed, and the back edge of the rig is pulled right in.

Finian Maynard, at one time the world's fastest windsurfer, in training for a speed-sailing event.

Speed Records

In the 1980s and 1990s, windsurfing boards were among the fastest sailcraft on the water. Recently, both sailboats and kitesurfers have been faster: in 2009, the sailboat *Hydroptère* managed a speed of 51.36 knots, or 95.12 kilometres per hour (59.10 miles per hour). At that time, the three fastest windsurfers ever were:

1. Antoine Albeau (France)   49.09 knots (90.91 kilometres per hour or 56.49 miles per hour)

2. Finian Maynard (British Virgin Islands)   48.70 knots (90.19 kilometres per hour or 56.04 miles per hour)

3. Patrik Diethelm (Italy)   46.57 knots (86.24 kilometres per hour or 53.59 miles per hour)

These world records were all set on a 500-metre (1640-foot) course at the French town of Saintes-Maries-de-la-Mer. The town has a strip of water known as "The French Trench", which was specially built for speed sailing on a windsurfing board.

The Speed World Cup usually starts in late March, in France. Then it moves around to other countries in Europe: Sweden, Greece, Germany, Austria, the UK, Holland and Ireland. You can track down events through the Speed World Cup website at www.speedworldcup.com.

SPEED-SAILING CENTRAL

The top locations for speed sailing world records are Saintes-Maries-de-la-Mer in France and Namibia, southern Africa. The Namibia records have been set either at the Lüderitz Speed Challenge in the town of Lüderitz, or at Walvis Bay Speed Week.

Lake Arenal

Lake Arenal must be one of the world's most unusual windsurfing locations. It was created when a hydroelectric dam was built in 1973. The lake is so big it took three years to fill up. Looming over one end is a huge volcano – which can sometimes be heard rumbling and grumbling in the background.

LAKE ARENAL
Location: Costa Rica
Type of sailing: flat-water, some small waves
Difficulty level: 2 of 5
Best season: all year

Tip from a Local
If it rains, it usually rains harder on the north side of the lake – so if you like the sunshine, stay on the south shore.

Lake Arenal's constant winds make it a great place for racing around doing jumps.

WHY LAKE ARENAL?
The lake covers 85 square kilometres (32.8 square miles), so somewhere on its shores there are conditions to suit everyone. For beginners, there are sheltered areas for practising hauling up the sail, plus turning round by **tacking** or **gybing**. For more experienced sailors, the wind blows stronger further out on the lake. On strong-wind days, there are even small waves for practising jumps.

If you like Lake Arenal...
... you could also try:
• Foca, Turkey
It has sheltered areas for practice.

WHEN ARE CONDITIONS BEST?

Beginners: From May to October there are lighter winds that are ideal for beginners. Windy days are less common, but if the wind drops off completely you can always visit the volcano. It's advertised as being "90 per cent safe"!

Improvers and experts: The lake is windiest from November to April, and this is when more experienced sailors head for Lake Arenal. On a few days a year the wind gets to over 80 kilometres per hour (49.7 miles per hour): only the real experts head out when this happens.

SKILL
Turning around

Turning around, so that you can get back to shore, is one of the most crucial skills in windsurfing, for obvious reasons. The easiest way to turn the board around is to tack.

1. Lean the mast backwards, so that the board heads up into the wind.

2. Step your front foot in front of the mast and bring your hands to the front of the boom.

3. Reach around the mast with your rear hand, to grip the boom on the other side of the sail.

4. Step around the mast and bring your other hand (which is now your rear hand) around too.

5. Lean the sail forwards so that the wind pulls the board right around. Sail away with a smile.

THE SECRET LANGUAGE OF WINDSURFING

tack turn with the nose of the board into the wind

gybe turn with the nose of the board away from the wind

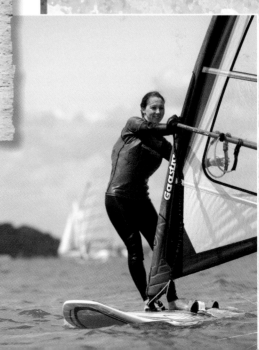

About a third of the way through a tack, this sailor is about to step around the mast and change direction.

Dahab

If you asked most windsurfers to describe their perfect sailing spot, they'd probably say:

- consistent winds of about 25 to 30 kilometres per hour (15.5 to 18.6 miles per hour)
- warm air and sea temperatures
- a variety of types of sailing, including flat-water and wave sailing.

Dahab has all three of these.

DAHAB
Location: Egypt
Type of sailing: flat-water, small waves
Difficulty level: 2.5 of 5
Best season: all year

It might look like a crash, but it isn't — this sailor is using Dahab's constant wind to practise his wave-sailing techniques.

If you like Dahab...

... you could also try:
- Porto Heli, Greece

It's good for planing.

WHY DAHAB?

Dahab is a sheltered bay on the coast of the Red Sea. Everything about the bay seems to have been designed for windsurfing. The wind blows in a direction that makes sure anyone who gets into difficulty is simply blown to a sandy beach. In winter, European windsurfers head here for the warm water and constant winds.

Tip from a Local

Dahab's winds are strongest in summer, when the desert temperatures are highest and pull air off the sea.

WHEN ARE CONDITIONS BEST?

Beginners: The calm, shallow water of the inner bay is ideal for beginners to practise in the morning.

Improvers: Further out in the bay it is windier, especially later in the day. Improvers can practise their turns and try little jumps in safety.

Experts: Outside the lagoon is a reef where the waves can reach 4 metres (13 feet) high. This is where the experts head for some wave sailing.

THE SECRET LANGUAGE OF WINDSURFING

across the wind at 90 degrees to the wind direction

SKILL
Planing and speed

"Planing" happens when a windsurfing board is going fast enough to skim along on top of the water like a speedboat, instead of ploughing through it like a canoe. Good sailors are quickly able to get their board planing:

1. At first, the board is sailing **across the wind**, but not planing.

2. The sailor leans forward and angles the mast slightly forwards. This steers the board downwind and gives it an extra boost of speed.

3. The extra burst of speed lifts the board on to the plane.

4. Once the board is skimming along, the sailor slowly angles the mast back, to come across the wind once more.

The board remains on the plane because it needs less power to stay on the plane than it did to start planing.

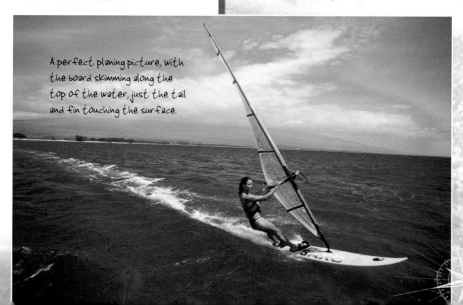

A perfect planing picture, with the board skimming along the top of the water, just the tail and fin touching the surface.

El Yaque

El Yaque is a windsurfing hotspot on the tiny Caribbean island of Margarita. During the northern winter, warm air, warm water, and a warm welcome bring windsurfers to the island from all round the world. From December until April, steady winds blow past the island and guarantee good windsurfing.

EL YAQUE
Location: Margarita Island, Venezuela
Type of sailing: flat-water, wind chop
Difficulty level: 2.5 of 5
Best season: November to May

WHY EL YAQUE?

El Yaque has a combination of lagoon sailing, where the water is rarely more than waist-deep, and open-ocean windsurfing. The water in the lagoon is so shallow that if you fall off, you can easily just jump back on the board. Further out, the **wind chop** gives experts a chance to practise their jumps.

THE SECRET LANGUAGE OF WINDSURFING

wind chop small, peaky waves thrown up by wind

freestyle using jumps, fast turns and spins of the sail

You can tell by the shape of the tops of the trees that the wind is blowing nicely in Margarita.

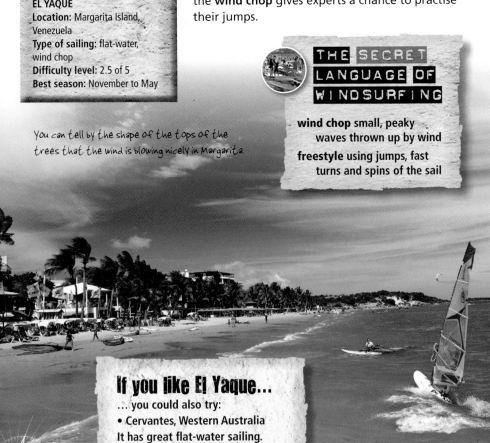

If you like El Yaque...

... you could also try:
• Cervantes, Western Australia
It has great flat-water sailing.

Tip from a Local
If the wind drops off, try surfing, diving or snorkelling.

This sailor is nicely hooked in and is letting the harness lines and the footstraps take the strain.

WHEN ARE CONDITIONS BEST?

Beginners: In the morning there are lighter winds of about 20 kilometres per hour (12.4 miles per hour), so conditions are great for beginners in the lagoon.

Improvers: Around lunchtime, the wind starts to pick up and improvers will head out on to the water. Smaller sails are needed because of the more powerful winds.

Experts: By about 3.00 p.m. the wind can reach 50 kilometres per hour (31 miles per hour). Expert sailors, riding small boards with small sails, head out on to the sea for some **freestyle** windsurfing.

In stronger winds, sailors use a harness to take some of the strain off their arms. The harness connects their body to the boom, and allows them to use their body weight to balance against the sail. When using a harness, sailors also wedge their feet into the footstraps on the deck of the board.

1. Only try to hook into the harness once the board is planing.

2. Pull the boom towards you, and lift your body slightly so that the harness lines hook on to the harness itself.

3. With your back knee bent, slide your front foot into the front footstrap. Then move your rear foot backwards and into one of the rear footstraps.

4. Let your weight go forwards, into the boom, to put pressure through the mast foot. This keeps the board flat and increases speed.

The Gorge

THE GORGE
Location: Washington/
Oregon, USA
Type of sailing: all types
Difficulty level: 3 of 5
Best season: April to November

Who says you don't get waves on rivers? This sailor seems to have found one at the Columbia River Gorge.

The Gorge is a world-famous windsurfing location with a difference – it's on a river, rather than the ocean or a lake. Its full name is the Columbia River Gorge. Winds blow along the gorge past the town of Hood River. The town has become a favourite stop-off for some of the world's best windsurfers.

WHY THE GORGE?

The Gorge has every kind of sailing (apart from wave sailing on open-ocean **swells**, of course). The wind blows more strongly in some spots than others. On the same day, improvers can be blasting to and fro at Home Valley, while a few kilometres away the experts are jumping large waves at Swell City.

Tip from a Local

The river barges on the Columbia River can't stop very quickly – it's best to stay well away from them unless you're an expert sailor.

If you like The Gorge...

... you could also try:
• River Rhine, Germany
It offers plenty of river-sailing thrills.

About a third of the way through a carved gybe, this sailor is about to let go with his rear hand and flip the rig around.

SKILL
carving gybes

Carved gybes are one of the techniques that mark out really good sailors. A carved gybe is one where the board makes a long, drawn-out turn without stopping planing.

1. The sailor takes his or her back foot out of the strap and turns the board downwind. It's important to keep the speed up.

2. A third of the way through the turn, the sail is out to the side as the board runs downwind. The rider's weight is in the centre of the board and his or her feet are out of both footstraps.

3. Halfway through the turn, still planing, the rider lets go with their rear hand. The sail flips round and the rider reaches across, grabs the boom with their free hand, and then transfers the other hand.

4. The rider then **sheets in**, getting the power on as shown in the technique feature on page 17. The board should keep planing and head off in the opposite direction.

THE SECRET LANGUAGE OF WINDSURFING

swell rolling ocean waves that come in to the beach in lines

sheet in pull the trailing end of the boom towards the board

WHEN ARE CONDITIONS BEST?

Beginners: The Gorge isn't ideal for complete beginners, but Home Valley in the mornings is not too windy and has calmer water.

Improvers: The area around the town of Hood River has small waves and good wind for intermediate sailors.

Experts: It's experts-only among the big waves and strong winds of Doug's Beach, Swell City or Rufus.

Tarifa

Tarifa sits on the very southern tip of Spain. Less than 20 kilometres (12.4 miles) away lies Africa's coast. When the wind comes from the south, you might hear the sound of the muezzin calling North African Muslims to their morning prayers. Mostly, though, the wind comes from the east or the west, channelled through the strip of water between Europe and Africa.

TARIFA
Location: Spain
Type of sailing: all types
Difficulty level: 3.5 of 5
Best season: all year

Tarifa is a popular spot, as this melée of windsurfers and kitesurfers shows. But there's plenty of wind and water to go around.

WHY TARIFA?

This is one of Europe's best, most popular windsurfing and kitesurfing destinations. It is almost always windy and, depending on which wind is blowing, conditions are good for different types of sailing. The Levante wind blows from the Mediterranean, and brings warm air and smooth seas. The Poniente blows from the Atlantic, and brings cooler air and rough seas.

Tip from a Local
The water off Tarifa is usually quite chilly, even in the middle of summer – you'll definitely need a wetsuit.

WHEN ARE CONDITIONS BEST?

Beginners: Tarifa's large, sand-bottomed bay is perfect for beginners in the morning.

Improvers: Around lunchtime, the wind starts to pick up and improvers head out into the bay.

Experts: Expert sailors wait for the strong Levante winds, or go wave sailing when the Poniente is blowing surf in from the Atantic.

THE SECRET LANGUAGE OF WINDSURFING

sheet out release the trailing edge of the boom so that the sail catches less wind

If you like Tarifa...

... you could also try:
• Paracuru, Brazil
It has great flat-water and wave sailing.

SKILL
Jumps: high or long?

Nothing beats the feeling of suddenly, silently flying through the air after you've done a jump! At first, people learn two main kinds of jump:

• Jumping high: the sailor picks a steep section of wave to launch the jump. As the board takes off, the sailor **sheets out** the sail. The board goes steeply up into the air, then comes back down to land on its tail. It almost (but not quite) floats down using the sail as a parachute.

• Jumping long: the sailor sheets out the sail, then as the board goes up the ramp, he or she sheets back in. The sailor then stays sheeted in through the air. The board carries on forwards, almost as if it is windsurfing through thin air. Most experts sheet out slightly as they land, to avoid the risk of landing nose-first and crashing.

He's looking for a safe landing – but it doesn't really seem as if there is one.

Essaouira

Essaouira is one of the oldest ports on Morocco's Atlantic coast. Here, travelling windsurfers get a chance to experience the ancient culture of North Africa – and some of the best windsurfing anywhere. Advanced sailors in particular flock here, because of the excellent wave sailing.

ESSAOUIRA
Location: Morocco
Type of sailing: all types
Difficulty level: 4 of 5
Best season: June to August is windiest; November to March has the biggest waves

WHY ESSAOUIRA?

Essaouira's long beach is partially sheltered from trade winds by the town. This is one of the things that make it such a great place for windsurfers. Beginners can sail in the area most protected from the wind. Experts can go further down the bay, where the wind blows harder and the waves pick up.

The town of Essaouira blocks some wind, and provides improvers with a bit of shelter. A little further down the coast, the sailing is for experts only.

If you like Essaouira...

... you could also try:
- **Deseado Estuary, Argentina**
It averages 300 windy days a year.

Not quite, but nearly – this sailor is just a split second away from landing this trick.

SKILL
Loops and barrel rolls

The technique that most clearly shows the difference between a good sailor and a really expert one is the loop.

- In a loop, the sailor does a jump, then flips with the board 360 degrees in the air, like a rollercoaster. The board lands back on the water pointing the same way as when it started.

There are two main variations of loop: forwards and backwards.

- The backwards loop, which used to be called a "barrel roll", is the easier of the two – although few people would actually call it easy.

- The forwards loop is like a forward roll through the air – while holding on to a windsurfing rig, with your feet in the footstraps. In fact, really expert riders sometimes take a foot out of the footstraps partway through the loop.

WHEN ARE CONDITIONS BEST?

Beginners: In the morning, there are lighter winds, so conditions are great for beginners in the sheltered parts of the bay.

Improvers and experts: Around lunchtime, the wind starts to increase. This happens because the desert behind the town gets hotter, pulling cool air off the sea and strengthening the wind. The effect is especially strong during the summer, when the sun is hottest.

Tip from a Local

Essaouira is famous for its pottery – it's good fun to explore the winding streets of the Safi area, where many potters have small shops.

Tiree Wave Classic

TIREE WAVE CLASSIC
Location: Tiree, Scotland
Type of sailing: wave
Difficulty level: 5 of 5
Contest held: October

Every October, the little ferry that travels to the tiny Scottish island of Tiree gets suddenly busy. The deck is unusually crowded, covered in camper vans and cars loaded up with brightly coloured windsurfing gear. The passengers are on their way to one of the longest-running wave-sailing contests around – the Tiree Wave Classic.

With so many good sailors around, finding a bit of air space for your loop can be tricky.

A BIT OF HISTORY

The Tiree Wave Classic was first held back in 1986. The event soon began to attract some of the world's top windsurfers. By 2007, the Wave Classic had become so successful that it became part of the World Cup, windsurfing's top level of competition.

WHY TIRE?

What is it that makes the world's best windsurfers willing to make the long trek up to Scotland's Western Isles? After all, most of them are used to warm seas and palm trees on the beach – not the chilly conditions of Scotland in October.

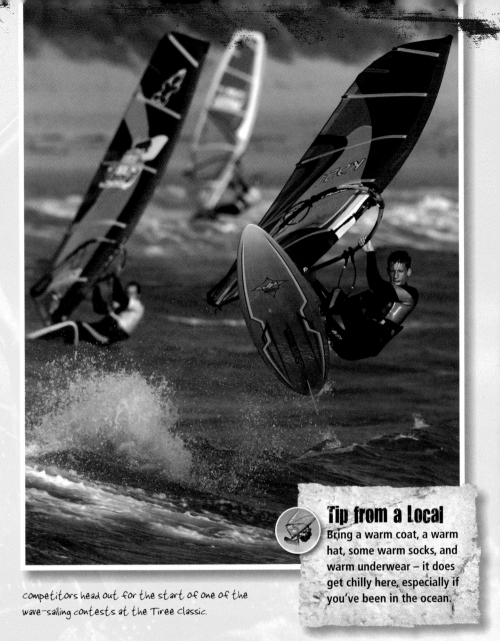

competitors head out for the start of one of the wave-sailing contests at the Tiree Classic.

Tip from a Local

Bring a warm coat, a warm hat, some warm socks, and warm underwear – it does get chilly here, especially if you've been in the ocean.

Tiree has three big attractions for windsurfers:
• The average wind speed is 27 kilometres per hour (16.8 miles per hour).
• In autumn, spring and winter, big surf rolls in from the Atlantic.

• The island gets the most sunshine of anywhere in the UK, and has long, beautiful white-sand beaches. The water is so blue you could imagine you're in the Caribbean (until your teeth start chattering).

Ho'okipa

Ho'okipa is a name that puts equal feelings of fear and excitement into the hearts of windsurfers the world over. Everyone who sails here has a story to tell: of half their equipment being smashed to pieces on the rocks, perhaps, or of the wind dying as a **set** of giant waves comes into view. This is not a place for the faint-hearted.

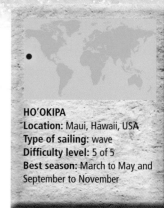

HO'OKIPA
Location: Maui, Hawaii, USA
Type of sailing: wave
Difficulty level: 5 of 5
Best season: March to May and September to November

Tip from a Local

Unless you are an expert sailor, the place to head on Maui is Kanaha, where the sheltered lagoon is great for all levels.

WHY HO'OKIPA?

Expert windsurfers come to Ho'okipa for one reason: the wave sailing. In spring and autumn, trade winds blow steadily and mast-high waves roll on to the reef. These conditions create a wave-sailor's playground. There are many hazards, though: sharp lava rocks, **rip currents**, and sudden drops in the wind in the area where waves break.

Hot wave-riding action from Ho'okipa, Hawaii.

If you like Ho'okipa...

..., you could also try:
• Margaret River, Western Australia
• Le Morne, Mauritrius
• Ponta Preta, Cape Verde
They all offer extreme wave-sailing action.

SKILL
Wave riding etiquette

WHEN ARE CONDITIONS BEST?
Beginners and improvers: Ho'okipa is not for sailors in these categories. Confident improvers might be able to sail along the coast at Spreckelsville, but even here the standard is usually very, very high.

Experts: The best times of year for big surf and trade winds are spring and autumn.

However you look at it, this is going to hurt. You have to be brave to sail at Ho'okipa.

Riding a windsurfing board in big waves is a dangerous business. Sailors have developed a set of rules to help make sure everyone stays as safe as possible:

• Sailors heading out through the waves have right of way. Someone surfing in, towards the beach, has to steer around them.

• One sailor per wave. If someone else is already riding a wave, leave them to it and look for another one.

• If more than one sailor tries to catch a wave, the upwind sailor (the one closest to where the wind is blowing from) has the right to ride the wave.

• Always be aware of other people in the water – sailors, surfers, kayakers and swimmers, for example – and make sure you steer a wide path around them.

THE SECRET LANGUAGE OF WINDSURFING

set group of waves that appear one after another, close together

rip current strong ocean current, caused when water pushed ashore by waves flows back out to sea

Glossary

WORDS FROM THE SECRET LANGUAGE FEATURES

across the wind at 90 degrees to the wind direction

blasting windsurfing at maximum speed

boom rail attached to the mast, which the sailor holds on to

deck top of a windsurfing board

flat-water sailing windsurfing on a lake or ocean with little or no waves

freestyle using jumps, fast turns and spins of the sail

gybe turn with the nose of the board away from the wind

kitesurfing watersport powered by a kite, with the sailor standing on a small, surfboard-like board

kook incompetent person

mast foot attachment between the mast and the deck

rig sail, mast and boom together

rip current strong ocean current, caused when water pushed ashore by waves flows back out to sea

sailor someone who does windsurfing or other kinds of sailing

set group of waves that appear one after another, close together

sheet in pull the trailing end of the boom towards the board

sheet out release the trailing edge of the boom so that the sail catches less wind

swell rolling ocean waves that come in to the beach in lines

tack turn with the nose of the board into the wind

uphaul rope attached to boom, used to pull sail from water

wave sailing windsurfing on rough water, particularly on ocean waves

wind chop small, peaky waves thrown up by wind

OTHER WORDS WINDSURFERS USE

clew corner of the sail furthest from the mast

leech imaginary straight line from the tip of the sail to the clew

leeward the side away from the wind

luffing flapping of the sail when the mast edge is pointing too much into the wind

newbie person who is new to windsurfing

offshore wind wind blowing away from the shore; dangerous for sailors, as it blows them out to sea

onshore wind wind blowing towards the shore

sea breeze wind that happens in the afternoon on hot days. As the land heats up, the warm air above it rises. Cooler air from above the sea rushes in to take its place, causing an onshore wind.

sideshore wind blowing across the shore

windward the side facing the wind

Finding Out More

THE INTERNET

www.boardseeker.com
This excellent Internet resource for windsurfers has video clips from big contests, travel advice, tests of equipment, interviews with top riders, advice on technique, and much more besides.

BOOKS

Radical Sports: Windsurfing Amanda Barker (Heinemann Library, 2000)

X-Treme Sports: Windsurfing Bob Italia and Stephanie F. Hedlund (Checkerboard Books, 2003)

Each of these children's books introduces the basic skills and techniques of windsurfing for beginners, and gives advice about equipment and clothing.

Windsurfing: The Essential Guide to Equipment and Techniques Simon Bornhoft (New Holland Publishers, 2004)
Although this is a book for adults as well as children, it is reasonably easy to follow. The author is a former top-level windsurfer, and has been a successful windsurfing coach for over 20 years.

MAGAZINES

Windsurf and *Boards*
These are the UK's two leading windsurfing magazines. Each carries articles about technique, equipment reviews, interviews with top-level sailors, and news about windsurfing competitions and the windsurfing industry. They also have websites at **www.windsurf.co.uk** and **www.boards.co.uk.**

Wind Surfing
This is one of the leading windsurfing magazines in the USA. It includes equipment tests, interviews, and other news, and takes a wider-ranging view than some other magazines, with articles from North America, Europe and the rest of the world. The magazine has a website at **www.windsurfingmag.com.**

Index